Penzance and Newlyn 1
Victorian Magic L:

At the end of the 19th century, there was a yearning for times past, when England's towns and cities were unpolluted by belching factory chimneys and the pace of life was slower. Some of the best Victorian photographers took and sold photographs which reflected this pre-industrial, perceived 'golden age' and the visual charms of Penzance, Newlyn and Mousehole provided suitable locations and subjects. Over one hundred years later, these photographs enable us to step back in time and experience fragmentary moments in the lives of our Victorian ancestors.

This booklet reproduces photographs from the Keasbury-Gordon Photograph Archive. Most of them were taken by Graystone Bird who won many awards for his photography but is now virtually unknown because of the 'forgotten' format in which his images were published ..... glass 'magic lantern' projection slides. The photos of Pilchard fishermen were taken by an amateur photographer in south west Cornwall but the precise location is unknown. The text is from a travel guide which was published in 1898. It is in two parts, a history and general description of Cornwall and a detailed exploration of the area between Penzance and Land's End, plus a note on pilchard fishing. The maps are from the same book.

The photographs and the text complement each other and enable us to travel back in time to visit this delightful corner of Victorian England. I hope you enjoy the journey.

Andrew Gill

The Magic Lantern

The magic lantern was the predecessor of the pre-digital slide projector. The first magic lanterns were made in the mid-1600s by natural philosophers (early scientists) who were exploring the nature and commercial potential of optics. Light sources and lenses improved throughout the 1700s and 1800s and, as a consequence, it was possible to show bigger, brighter and clearer pictures to ever larger audiences. During Queen Victoria's reign, magic lantern shows became established as mass-media entertainment. Shows could be lavish, theatrical events with all the razzmatazz of today's TV talent contests, with multiple lanterns to produce special effects. Magic lanterns were also used in Church and village halls and educational establishments for talks and lectures and, of course, in ordinary homes for family entertainment.

Some slides gave the illusion of movement. These included colourful kaleidoscopes, children skipping, a dentist pulling teeth and a man swallowing rats as he sleeps with his mouth open ...... still a favourite with children (of all ages) who attend my magic lantern shows!

In the early 1800s, magic lanterns were used to create phantasmagoria horror shows, where terrifying devils, witches and the grim reaper were conjured out of thin air, with accompanying sound effects, in suitably scary venues. These shows employed the latest technology and created sophisticated illusions to entice customers to part with their money and be scared out of their wits.

Magic lantern slides were made of glass. Early ones were hand painted and expensive to produce and buy but, from the mid-1800s, photographic images were applied to slides, mass-production followed and the magic lantern industry boomed. In its heyday, the 1890s, millions of slides were made, particularly in Britain, France and America, for entertainment, amusement, education, spiritual enlightenment and moral crusades.

In Britain, manufacturers of lantern slides produced sales catalogues of individual and sets of slides that could be purchased or hired by mail-order or from local, high-street outlets. Photographic slides produced by Graystone Bird were critically acclaimed then and much admired by collectors now.

Graystone Bird was born in Somerset in 1862. His father, Frederick Charles Bird, ran a successful photographic business in Frome and in 1866 opened a new studio in Milsom Street, Bath. Around the age of fifteen, Graystone was apprenticed to his father to learn the technicalities of photography and the skills necessary for him to inherit the family business, the core of which was portrait photography. By the early 1890s, the business was producing a growing range of magic lantern slides, from photographs taken by Graystone. By 1896 he had succeeded his father as the proprietor of the business. He was an astute businessman and as well as selling photographs direct to the public from the Milsom Street shop and by mail-order, he also licensed other slide producers to use his images. Graystone promoted his business by attending photographic exhibitions. He won over two hundred prizes for individual photographs, including awards from international exhibitions in Vienna and Chicago and his work was recognised in America, Canada, Australia and Switzerland.

Graystone's slides are instantly recognisable by their unique style. They are very sharp with fine tone and contrast and often include people in artistic poses. Today, they form an important historical record of life in the communities that he photographed including Whitby, the Isle of Man, Castle Combe in Wiltshire and St. Ives and Newlyn. He died in 1943.

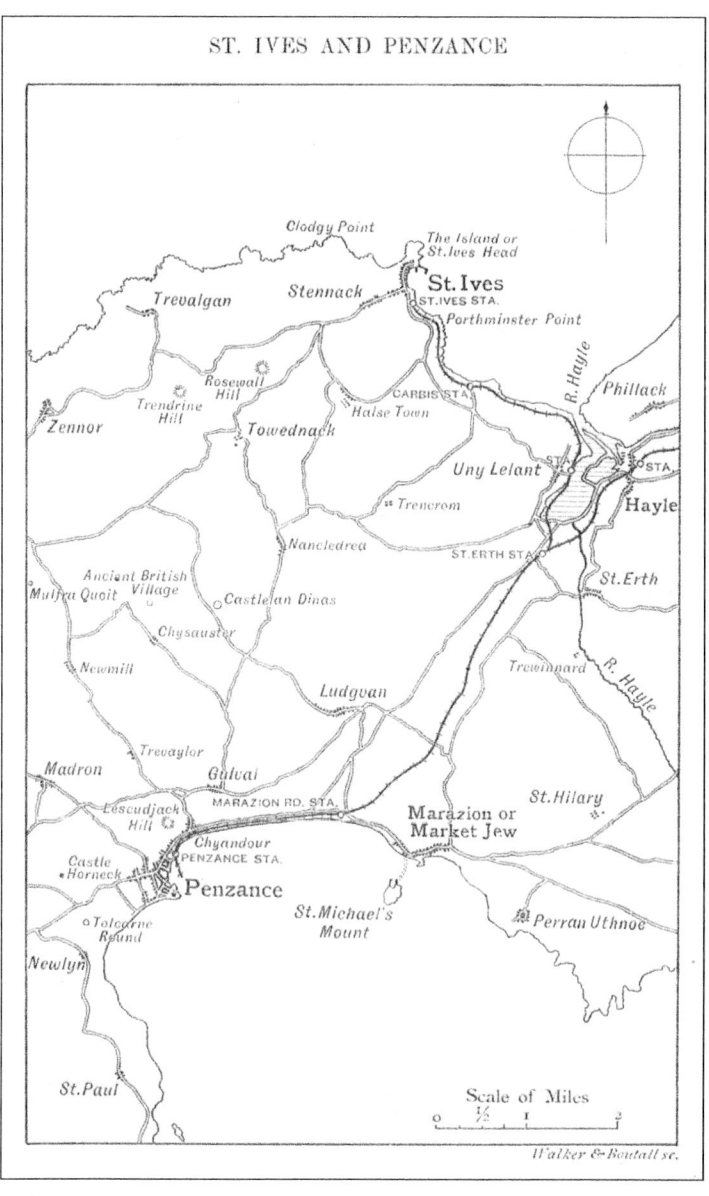

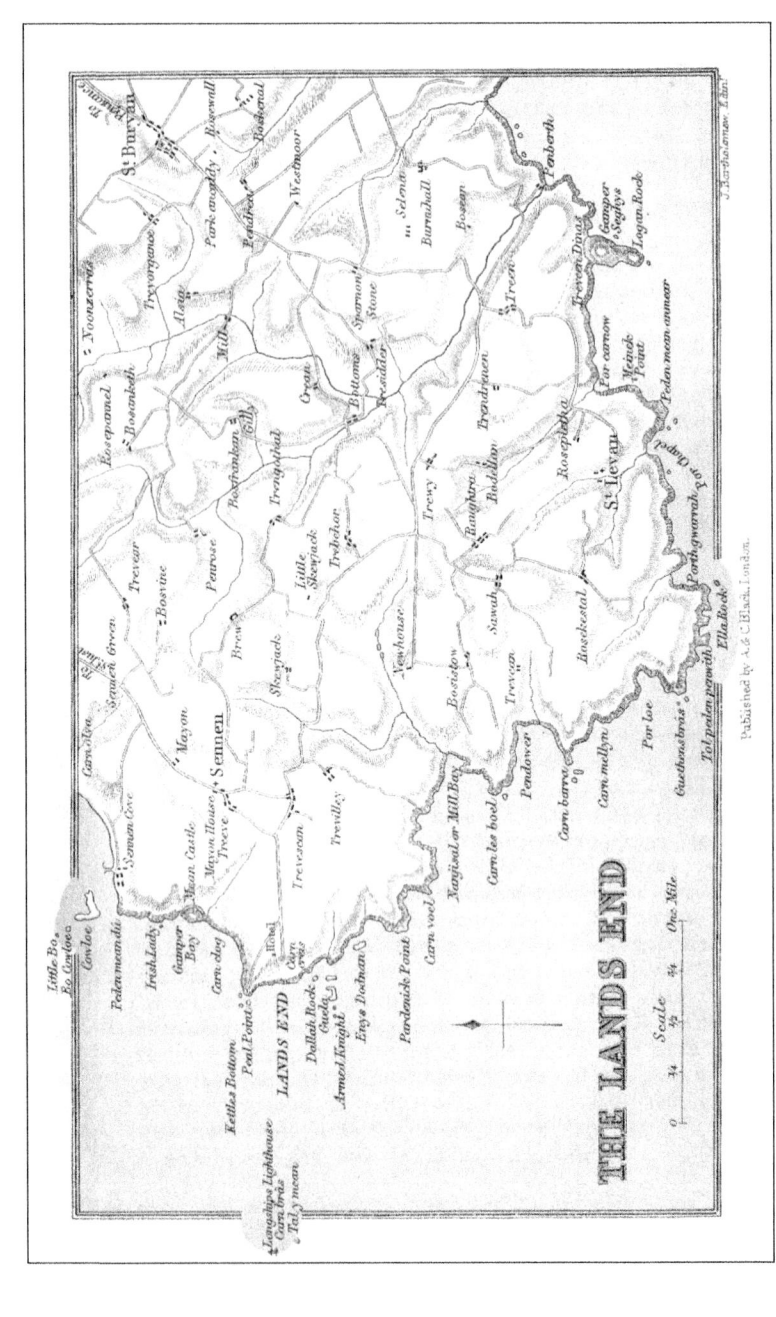

Penzance Harbour

The Esplanade, Penzance

The Quay, Penzance

The Esplanade, Penzance

Penzance

St. Michael's Mount

Fishing boats in Mounts Bay

St. Michael's Mount

The following fifteen photographs are of Newlyn

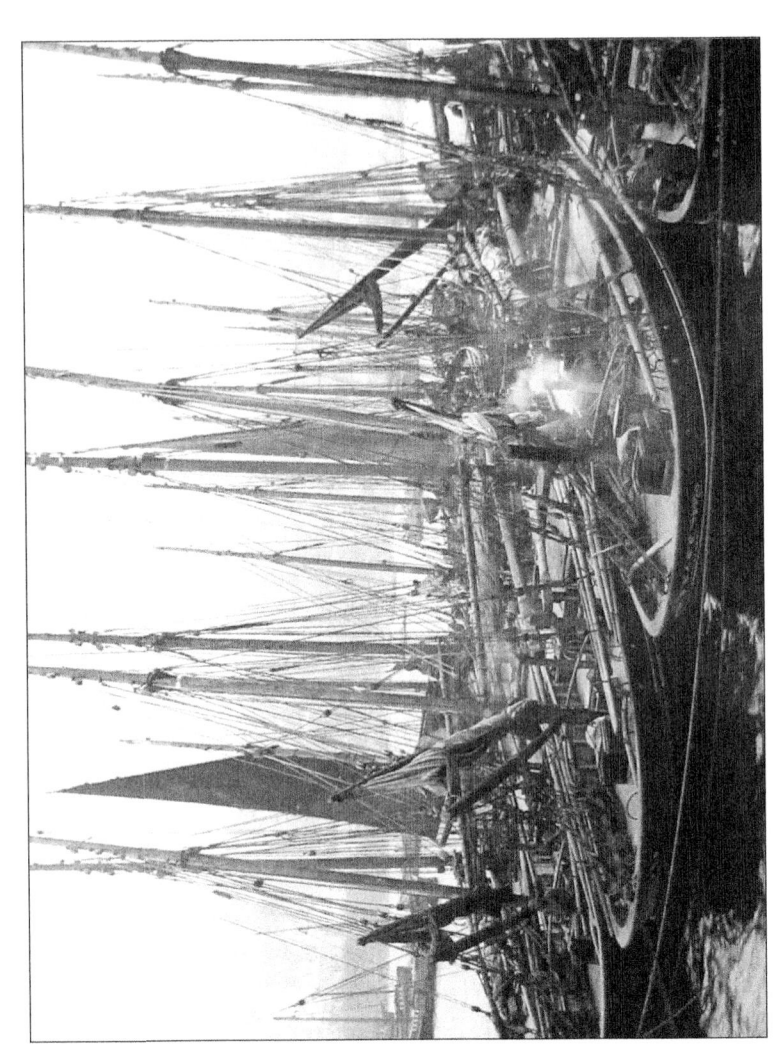

Newlyn

Mousehole

Mousehole

Longships Lighthouse off Lands End

Pilchard fishing using a seine net (and the three photographs on next page)

INTRODUCTION

The "Duchy of Cornwall," as this south-western appendix of England loves to be styled, is a country of markedly individual characteristics, distinguishing it from all other parts of the kingdom. Many strangers crossing the Tamar, "over that fairy bridge of Brunel's, hung aloft between the blue of the river and the blue of the sky," are fain to fancy themselves in another country; and as they advance, it is to find that impression deepened which gives a Cornish tour something of the interest of foreign travel. Truth to tell, this interest is mainly confined to the broken and wave-beaten coast-line, almost uniformly striking, and often magnificent, broken by frequent fishing havens that to more than one sense suggest the kind of picturesqueness looked for under a Mediterranean sky. Inland, the scenery, dear as it may be to those who have known it from childhood, is apt to affect the unfamiliar eye as dreary in its monotonous expanse of rough brown moors, swelling up into low ridges, scarred by mines and topped by smokeless engine-shafts to take the place of trees—"a most unclassical Campagna, covered with the ruins of obscure industry." Even the dignity of height is wanting here, Brown Willy, the loftiest point in Cornwall, being under 1400 feet.

Cornwall's jovial neighbours are in the way of asserting that it does not grow wood enough to make a coffin. This of course is a calumny; but timber here has to be sought for in the sheltered hollows, often nourishing a thick growth of oak-coppice, as well as statelier trees, among them the small-leaved Cornish elm, so rarely found in

INTRODUCTION

other counties. On the open heights, flowering its best at that season when, as poets tell us, kissing comes most in favour, glows a profusion of gorse, including the double-blossomed sort, which, with the various heaths, the white *erica vagans* and the *ciliaris* their peculiar pride, and the splendid cliff-carpeting of the sea pink, the hardy bloom of brambles, and the graceful verdure of tamarisks in warm nooks, as well as the stains of lichen upon hoary rocks, themselves often finely tinted, go far to relieve the prevailing dulness of colour. Brick appears rarely where its becoming background of green is wanting; but white-wash is much used, with lively effect, on the open landscapes. The stair-like Cornish stiles, the substantial walls and hedges, the conical "windmow" stacks, the prominence of church towers and other beacon marks, are striking features on the face of the country.

The time when Cornwall is seen to the best advantage is perhaps in spring, which here comes to meet one from the Atlantic; or in late autumn, while a hectic glow still lingers about "the good gigantic smile o' the old brown earth." Those who love the "high midsummer pomps" might feast their eyes more fully elsewhere. In winter this scenery suffers less than that of most other parts. As the question of weather is a most important one to tourists, we will begin with it in sketching the qualities of a district which gets more than its fair share of what wind and rain are going in our island.

The **Climate** of Cornwall is the most equable on the British mainland, owing to the manner in which this tongue of land, almost surrounded by sea, is washed by the Gulf Stream and brushed by the prevalent south-west winds. The southern end, less exposed to other influences, is remarkably mild in winter and not often hot in summer, the usual range of temperature being about 20°. Snow and frost seldom hold out long against the mild breath of the Atlantic; yet, now and again natives are surprised and strangers disappointed by a visitation of exceptional severity, as in the spring blizzard of 1891 and the long

INTRODUCTION

hard winter of 1895. Such a climate has the defects of its qualities; it takes all the bracing force of sea air to save it from being relaxing in its humid softness, which, indeed, seems not to hurt the health of those born under its mists and clouds. Tourists, taking one month with another, must reckon at least every second day as likely to be more or less wet, and will be lucky not to come in now and then for a week of rain; but all the more clear and lovely are the glimpses of sunshine, for which, in winter, Cornwall has a good chance of being better off than its neighbours. As hinted above, the sea winds prevent timber trees from reaching any great size in open situations; but lower growths show singular luxuriance in sheltered nooks, especially of the south coast. About Falmouth and Penzance, and in the Scilly Isles, several varieties of palms, cacti, and camellias, and other exotics flourish under the open air. The olive tree has been planted with success in a few places. The Austrian pine, and other foreigners of this species, do well in the western parts. Stone fruit, however, and apples and pears, do not generally gain the same full flavour as in Devon, for want of dry heat.

Geology.—The Carbonaceous formations of North Devon extend into the north-western angle of the county, but by far the greater part of Cornwall belongs to the Devonian or greywacke series of rocks, consisting of slates and shales, which occupy much of South Devon, and occur again in North Devon and Somersetshire. From the Devonians four large patches of granite project at intervals. The Land's End district forms the most westerly of these granite patches. A large mass of serpentine occupies the district about the Lizard Head; and the Devonian rocks are traversed by numerous veins and outbreaks of trap and of "elvan,"—the name locally given to porphyries, granitic and felspathic. But to a great extent the cliffs are of slate, taking on a grimly bristling roughness under the lashing of the waves, especially along the storm-beaten walls of the north-west coast-line.

INTRODUCTION

Of the mineral veins, for which Cornwall has so long been famous, tin is found in both granite and slate ; copper for the most part in granite. The most important Cornish copper ore is the sulphuret, commonly known as grey ore by the miners ; but copper pyrites, or the bisulphuret of copper, occurs far more frequently in both Cornwall and Devon. The tin of Cornwall has been known and worked from a period long before the dawn of certain history. Copper, which lies deeper in the earth, and consequently cannot be "streamed" for, was almost unnoticed in the county until the end of the 15th century, and little attention was paid to it until the last years of the 17th. No mine seems to have been worked exclusively for copper before the year 1700 ; soon after which a Mr. Coster gave great impulse to the industry by draining some of the deeper mines, and instructing the men in an improved method of dressing the ore.

Unfortunately, the Cornish mines have been steadily decaying in value of late years. In every sense they are going down, and the deeper the workings the more expensive it becomes to bring up the metal, while in other parts of the world their rivals are in the position of our early miners, who got their easy gains near the surface. For the tin trade, Cornwall finds its chief competitor in the Straits Settlements, where the mineral is abundant and the labour cheap. As there, moreover, payments are received in gold, and expenses mainly paid in depreciated silver, the vexed controversy of bimetallism comes in to trouble the heads of Cornish-village politicians. Another much disputed question is as to attracting outside capital by making the mines into Limited Liability Companies. At present most of them are mainly owned in the neighbourhood, and often in small shares, which spread the interest in their prosperity and give honest Cornishmen something of the excitement without the guilt of gambling. This diffused speculation is quite a feature of the local character ; it has been said that nearly every Cornishman feels certain of being descended from King Arthur and of being destined to make his fortune in a mine, as so many have done

INTRODUCTION

before him. Fortunes are not made in mines nowadays; and, as one and the other comes to be "knacked," the loss is at once felt in the locality, both directly and indirectly. Copper is even in a worse plight than tin. The only industries of the kind doing at all well at present are the granite quarries, and the china clay workings in the centre of the county. The fisheries, too, that second string to Cornwall's bow, are not what they once were. A people singularly attached to their own soil, find themselves, then, more and more obliged to emigrate. Cornish miners turn up all over the world, now in South America, helping to ruin their old country, now behind the walls of Lucknow, throwing down the musket for the pick and recalling their old trade to baffle the sapping of the wily sepoy. Thus the population has been steadily thinning, till at the last census it numbered less than 318,600, over an area of nearly 1350 square miles, a decrease of 50,000 in one generation. In the mining districts, where this population groups thickest, it is drawn into clusters which here and there run together without rounding themselves off with municipal dignity, unless they go to swell some former nucleus of intercourse. No town in Cornwall contains more than about 15,000 inhabitants; and even then this figure is reached by counting in straggling suburbs that can hardly be distinguished from large independent villages. On purely agricultural land, the population is more disseminated, as on the coast, where, however, it gathers every few miles into snug fishing villages, while the "church town" of large moorland parishes may be a mere hamlet.

The Geology of Cornwall has thus had such an influence on its progress that we are led into considerations which might appropriately have followed a sketch of its history, when we pass to man from nature.

History.—Cornwall, like the rest of England, is first found inhabited by a Celtic race, who may here have supplanted a still older stock. In such a familiar feature as the saffron with which Cornishmen still love to colour their cakes, enthusiastic antiquaries have seen a touch of early

INTRODUCTION

Oriental intercourse; but we have no authentic knowledge of this country until after the Roman conquest of Britain. It remains uncertain whether Phœnician or Carthaginian traders actually visited the "Cassiterides," or whether they obtained their supplies of tin through Gaul. But we know that the tin of the district was largely exported from a very early period, and that the mines were still worked under the Romans. Cornwall formed part of the British Kingdom of Damnonia, which long resisted the advance of the Saxons westward, and remained almost unbroken in power until the reign of Ine of Wessex (688-726). From that time the borders of the British Kingdom gradually narrowed, until, about the year 926, Athelstan drove the Britons from Exeter, and fixed the Tamar as the limit between them and the Saxons of Devon. So at least say some authorities, while others place the boundary on a line between Plymouth and Tintagel, and reduce Athelstan's exploit to driving back a fresh Celtic irruption, perhaps made in alliance with the Danes. The British bishop, Conan, submitted to Archbishop Wulfhelm of Canterbury after Athelstan's conquest, and was reappointed by him in 936. The Cornish see was afterwards merged in that of Crediton, then in 1050 the place of the united sees was transferred to Exeter, where it remained till 1876. Cornwall, although the mass of the people remained Celtic, speedily received Saxon masters, and in the Domesday Survey the recorded names of the owners of land are all Saxon. The Conqueror bestowed nearly the whole county on his half-brother, Robert of Mortain, and thus arose the Earldom of Cornwall, which, considered too important a possession to be held by any one under royal rank, came to be an appanage of the heir-apparent to the crown. In 1336 the earldom was raised to a Duchy by Edward III. in favour of his son, the Black Prince, and of his heirs, eldest sons of the Kings of England. Since that time the Prince of Wales has always been Duke of Cornwall. The Duchy originally included Dartmoor Forest; and its income is at present derived from lands in Somerset and Devon as well as in Cornwall itself. The history of the Duchy is

INTRODUCTION

virtually that of Cornwall. There has been little to connect it with the general annals of the country except for rebellions under the Tudors, and during the Civil War, when Cornwall was for the most part royalist. Besides much skirmishing, there were two important battles within its bounds, that of Braddock Down (Jan. 19, 1642-3), and that of Stratton (May 15, 1643), both gained for the King. The more important histories of the county embrace Carew's *Survey of Cornwall*, Drew's *History of Cornwall*, Hal's *Parochial History of Cornwall*, Polwhele's *History of Cornwall*. Among recent works on the subject are Daniell and Collins's *History of Cornwall*, the *Church History of Cornwall*, and the *Parochial History* published by Mr. Lake.

Antiquities.—No part of England preserves so many antiquities of the primæval period. These chiefly abound in the district between Penzance and the Land's End, but they occur in all the wilder parts of the county. They may be classed as follows:—(1) *Cromlechs*. These in the west of Cornwall are called "quoits," with a reference to their broad and flat covering stones. The largest and most important are those known as Lanyon, Caerwynen, Mulfra, Chun, and Zennor quoits, all in the Land's End district. Of these Chun is the only one which has not been thrown down. Zennor is said to be the largest in the British Isles, while Lanyon, when perfect, was of sufficient height for a man on horseback to ride under. Of those in the eastern part of Cornwall, Trethevy near Liskeard and Pawton in the parish of St. Breock are the finest, and have remained intact. (2) Rude uninscribed *monoliths* are common to all parts of Cornwall. Those at Boleit, in the parish of Buryan, are perhaps the most important. (3) *Circles*, none of which are of great dimensions. The principal are the Hurlers, near Liskeard; the Boskednan, Boscawen-un, and Tregeseal circles; and that called the Dawns-un, or Merry Maidens. All of these, except the Hurlers, are in the Land's End district. Other circles that may be mentioned are the "Trippet Stones," in the Parish of Blisland, and one at Duloe.

INTRODUCTION

(4) Long *alignments* or *avenues* of stones, resembling those on Dartmoor, but not so perfect, are to be found on the moors near Roughtor and Brown Willy. A very remarkable monument of this kind exists in the neighbourhood of St. Columb, called the "Nine Maidens." It consists of nine rude pillars placed in a line, while near them is a single stone known as the "Old Man." (5) *Hut dwellings*. Of these there are at least two kinds, those in the eastern part of the county resembling the beehive structures and enclosures of Dartmoor, and those in the west, comprising "hut-clusters," having a central court, and a surrounding wall often of considerable height and thickness. The beehive masonry is also found in connection with these latter, as are also (6) *Caves*, or subterraneous structures, resembling those of Scotland and Ireland. (7) *Cliff castles* are a characteristic feature of the Cornish coast, as for example the "Little Dinas" near Falmouth, Trevalgue, near St. Columb, and Treryn, Mên, Kenidjack, Bosigran, and others in the west. These are all fortified against the land side. (8) *Hill castles*, or camps, are very numerous. Castle-an-Dinas, near St. Columb, is the best example of the earthwork camp, and Chun Castle, near Penzance, of the stone.

One of the most difficult problems of British archæology is to fix the epoch and race to which these prehistoric remains belong. The old theory of the days of Dr. Borlase and his followers, that they are Druidical, is now obsolete. The tendency of modern research is to throw their date back into a remote past long anterior to Julius Cæsar's conquest of Britain and the Christian era. Possibly they belong to an age before the arrival of even the Celts into Western Europe.

Of early Christian and mediæval antiquities the most noticeable are crosses, scattered all over the county, and of various dates, from the 6th to the 16th century, many resembling the early crosses of Wales; inscribed sepulchral stones of the 7th and 8th centuries, of which the "Mên scryffa" in Madron is a good example; and oratories of the Early Irish type like St. Pirans. This county is particularly

INTRODUCTION

well off for holy wells, whose wonder-working virtues are still not forgotten by a half-believing, half-jesting generation; and beside these wells are often found the ruins of ancient baptisteries consecrated by the shadowy memory of some saint. It is well known how rich Cornwall was in local saints —St. Piran, St. Nectan, St. Morwenna, St. Juliot, St. Eval, St. Ervyn, and countless others, whose names are hardly met with beyond its border. Almost every letter of the alphabet forms an initial in the peculiar nomenclature of Cornish parishes. The churches, for the most part, belong to the Perpendicular style, and show a simplicity in keeping with their surroundings. They are generally low in the body, but with high and plain granite towers. The rich tower of Probus, however, is an exception, and that of St. Austell, as well as the Church of St. Mary Magdalene at Launceston, the exterior of which is covered with sculpture. A peculiar feature found in several instances is a campanile or separated belfry. Within, the chief local characteristic is the absence of a chancel arch.

The castles of Launceston, Trematon, and Restormel seem to be of the time of Henry III., but the mounds which occur in the first two are no doubt much earlier, —possibly marking British strongholds. Tintagel has but a few shapeless walls. St. Michael's Mount, although castellated at an early period, has nothing more ancient than the 15th century. Pendennis, Star Fort, and others, are of Tudor date.

Language.—Of the Celtic tongues, Cornish and Armoric (the dialect of Brittany in France) resembled each other more than either of them did Welsh, nor is this the only trace of a connection which geographical situation has made natural.

The literary remains are very scanty. The old Cornish language was spoken till the 18th century, still surviving in a few fishing and mining terms, as in names of persons and places, "Pol, Tre, and Pen." The last sentence of the language used by the fishermen of Mount's Bay seems

INTRODUCTION

to have been "*Breal meta truja peswartha*—all is scrawed all along the line O." This mixed Cornish and English was used in living memory. The numerals (also remembered by a few in Newlyn and Mousehole) are :—

1. Un.	4. Padzher.	8. Eith.
2. Du.	5. Pemp.	9. Nau.
3. Tri.	6. Wheth.	10. Deig.
	7. Seith.	

The Cornish of our day are a mixed race, mainly Celtic, well made and sturdy in form. As in Ireland, the aristocracy has been largely of Norman or Saxon origin; but these grafts have quickly taken the qualities of the old stock; and here, as in Ireland, there seems something in the soil or the air to make intruders soon become *Cornubiensibus Cornubiensiores*. For Cornishmen are strongly marked by clannishness of an even more accentuated type than that found in west-countrymen generally, and seem to regard their fellow-subjects over the Tamar almost as foreigners. "Going to England" is the phrase with one who leaves his native county. The character of the people has been strongly tempered by the exciting pursuits of mining and fishing, not to speak of smuggling and wrecking practices that held out here after civilisation had tamed the lawless instincts of their neighbours. Even in this century the inhabitants of the Cornish coast proved hard to teach that a wreck was not fair game; and dark stories are told of how a ship would actually be enticed unto destruction on this cruel shore, that human vultures might gather to her plunder. The grandsons of those wreckers now man the lifeboats; yet something of the old Adam still seems to run in their blood, for it is said that a Cornishman will work harder and for less wages upon a wreck than at any other job. A rough population it must have been among whom John Wesley came, and found here an arena for an inspiring struggle with the devil. The results of his labours are well known; probably the hottest Churchman will admit that Methodism has been a regenerating force, through which a people not easily tamed have become remarkably sober and orderly. Other forms of dissent

INTRODUCTION

flourish, notably the Bryanite or Bible Christian sect, which has its stronghold in this corner of the country. On the other hand, the Established clergy, by a natural movement of repulsion, are apt to lean towards the High Church side. It should be said that an imaginative temperament gives a strong tinge of superstition to Cornish religion ; but stirring devotion here seems to have a wholesomely practical effect.

One point may be confidently insisted on : if Cornish clannishness is quick to resent the intrusion of outsiders in business, the idle stranger may be assured of friendly civility. His Celtic blood, and his independent pride, make every Cornishman more or less a gentleman ; so there is no part of England where the manners of all classes leave so little to be desired. We have used the word civility ; but that poorly expresses the hearty kindliness with which a visitor will find himself welcomed and furthered, so long as he remember not to abuse goodwill, to despise well-meant efforts, or to insult prejudice. Few who make their holiday quarters in Cornwall but come back with a warm memory of the honest solicitude of some motherly hostess, the untutored courtesy of some boatman, the rough willingness of some miner or labourer who has turned aside to help the bewildered wayfarer. Here indeed it seems that—

" Stranger is a holy name ;
Rest and a guide, and food and fire,
In vain he never must require."

While the temptation of gain, and continued commerce with those who place the heart in the purse, have done something to sophisticate some Cornwall hostelries, there are others where one is amazed that so little advantage is taken of opportunity to tax a visitor for entertainment offered as if "all for love and nothing for reward." And if some of these lodgings for travellers be not over-luxurious in their accommodations, we have good authority for holding that better is a dinner of tough fowls and plainly cooked herbs, under certain circumstances, than a *table d'hôte* menu and a host of Swiss waiters whose attentions

INTRODUCTION

become overpowering at the moment of payment. One who can fare on Cornish cream and Cornish cakes will find himself always at home here, nor, if his coming be expected, will he go without more solid repasture. But should his lot be cast in farm or cottage, a tender soul must harden himself against the draughts of fresh air likely to be freely supplied at most seasons of the year.

The backbone of travelling in this county is the Great Western Railway, which runs from Plymouth to Penzance, with branches to the narrow limits on either side. In the north part its rival, the London and South-Western Company, has taken an inch that may before long become an ell. The adventurous Cornishmen were early in welcoming railways with Celtic impulsiveness, but had not always counted the cost with Saxon prudence, so some side lines will be seen lying idle, overgrown with rust and grass, and others that are used only for the conveyance of minerals. The diffused grouping of the population leads to the railway communication being supplemented by many local coaches, omnibuses, and queer caravans, most of which find no place in imperial time-tables, but might often prove helpful to the leisurely traveller. The cyclist need not fear to be often brought to a stand here, though he must duly beware of abrupt steeps and rugged moorland tracks. One way or other the tourist will have little difficulty in getting about Cornwall; but this is a county the best points of which cannot be so well seen as by the pilgrim who with staff and scrip—not to say waterproof and stoutish sandals—fares sturdily on foot. To "One and all," as the Cornish motto has it, we wish *bon voyage*; and, we hope, have done our best to make the wish no idle compliment.

Penzance to Land's End

MARAZION.

HOTELS.—*Godolphin, Marazion*—*St. Michael's* Boarding-House (on the road from the station).

This venerable town is locally known as *Market Jew*, from which it has been supposed an ancient Jewish colony. The connection of Jews with Cornwall is an old story: a legend among metal workers represents Joseph of Arimathæa as engaged in the tin trade, travelling between Phœnicia and the Cassiterides, where it is even said that he brought the boy Jesus. But nowadays there are scholars who doubt if Jews were ever settled in Cornwall, and laugh away as a corruption the name *Jews' houses* given here and elsewhere to old smelting places; then the fanciful etymology of *Marah Zion* ("bitter Zion") is brought down to the plain prose of an old Cornish word for market. *St. Michael's Mount* may put in a very probable claim to be the *Ictis* of the ancient tin trade. More shadowy seems the location here of *Lyonnesse* and the scene of Arthur's great battle. Marazion was certainly a considerable place in old days, flourishing both as a port and as a goal of pilgrimage. But after serious losses from a French attack in

Longships Lighthouse off Land's End

MARAZION

Henry VIII.'s reign, and during the Cornish insurrection of 1549, it never recovered its importance, gradually falling into the shade of its former dependency, Penzance. Now little better than a big village, it has a modified prosperity in the concourse of summer lodgers, but rather of excursionists and tourists who visit it from more successful resorts. The winter climate of Marazion is one of the most genial in Cornwall; and this, with its pleasant situation, might well bring visitors to stay longer than a few hours. On the whole the place strikes one as more dignified and less dirty than most fishing villages of this coast. The one winding street has been a good deal smartened out of its antiquity. About its most open part, opposite St. Michael's Mount, will be found the chief buildings,—the Hotels, the *Post Office*, next door to which is an *Institute* with reading-room, lecture hall, etc.; then, on the other side, the most pretentious edifice in the town, the ground-floor occupied by a bank, the rest by municipal offices. Close at hand is the harbour, and the head of the causeway leading over to a tiny suburb at the foot of the Mount—the Acropolis and Alhambra of Marazion.

St. Michael's Mount is a rugged conical peak over 200 feet, insulated at high water, and commanding the waters of Mount's Bay from the Lizard to the Rundlestone. As in the case of its grander Breton namesake, it has long been crowned by a monastic fortress, now enlarged and adapted as the castellated mansion of Lord St. Levan.

The legend runs that it was originally enclosed by a great forest. Its Cornish name, indeed, is *Caraclowse in Cowse*, "the gray Rock in the Wood," which seems an awkward circumstance for the *Ictis* Island theory. The sacred character with which the Mount's imposing position naturally invested it is very ancient. To an anchorite who had fixed here his solitary dwelling, the Archangel Michael himself appeared,—hence Milton's allusion to "the great vision of the guarded mount." St. Keyne, in the 5th century, journeyed hither from Ireland. Some rude defences protected its steep at a very early date, for Edward the Confessor's charter, in 1047, to the Benedictine monks, whom he settled here, expressly grants its *castella* and other buildings. After the Conquest the Gilbertines took the place of the Benedictines, and their cell was attached by Robert, Earl of Cornwall, to the Abbey of St. Michael, on the coast of Normandy. The resemblance of St.

PENZANCE AND THE LAND'S END

Michael's Mount in Cornwall to that of Normandy is striking, and their historical connection certain. As an alien religious house the Cornish monastery was confiscated by Edward III. in his war with France, and afterwards bestowed upon Sion Nunnery, in Middlesex. In 1533, its site and revenues were granted to Humphrey Arundell of Laherne, who forfeited them in 1549. In Charles the Second's reign the estate was purchased of the Basset family by the St. Aubyns, who remain its owners.

All through the ages of faith, this was famed as a shrine and a sanctuary, besides playing its part as a stronghold. During the absence of Richard I. in Palestine, one Henry de Pomeroy having murdered a king's messenger, fled hither, dispossessed the monks, and held the hill on behalf of John Sansterre. But on Cœur de Lion's return, he was compelled to surrender, and to prevent himself from falling into the enraged monarch's hands, opened his veins and bled to death, or, according to another account, leapt his horse off the rock into the sea. The Earl of Oxford, flying from the battle of Barnet, *temp.* Henry VI., obtained admission in the disguise of a pilgrim, and, assisted by several of his followers, raised the Lancastrian standard, then made so stout a defence, it was deemed advisable to bribe him with a pardon upon condition that he yielded up the castle (A.D. 1471). Another refugee was Lady Catherine Gordon, the "Fair Rose of Scotland," and the beautiful wife of Perkin Warbeck; but she was soon torn from her sanctuary by Lord Daubeny. During the religious commotions which desolated Cornwall and Devonshire in 1549, the insurgents crossed the sands at low water, and, sheltering themselves under trusses of hay, climbed to the assault. They captured the castle, soon afterwards re-captured by the royalists, when Humphrey Arundell, the rebel leader, was beheaded. And, finally, its royalist garrison, under Sir Francis Basset, was compelled, during the Civil War, to surrender to a body of Parliamentarian troopers under Colonel Hammond. The Mount was visited by Charles II., and in 1846 by Queen Victoria, whose footprint upon the pier is marked by an inlaid brass.

St. Michael's Mount is reached from Marazion by boat, or at low water (8 hours out of the 24) by a paved causeway, 1200 feet long. There is a steamer several times a day (in summer) from Penzance. A fishing hamlet (*St. Aubyns Arms Inn*) lies about the small harbour and pier, above which rises the precipitous rock. The body is of granite, resting, on the north side, on a substratum of

MARAZION

slate, and streaked on the south-east by veins of glittering quartz. Beside the causeway will be seen an insulated mass of greenstone, on which a chapel once made the first station of pilgrims.

The entrance is through the Lodge and by a winding path and steps as avenue to a platform defended by two small batteries. The old Cross before which so many a knee has been bent, will be seen outside the chapel. In the castle itself the chief sight is the ancient Hall, now called the *Chevy Chace Room*, enriched with a cornice representing the fox, stag, boar, wild bull, and other hunting emblems ; also some old furniture, and trophies from the Soudan brought back by a member of the family. Among the portraits there are two by *Opie*. It is Lord St. Levan's wish that no payment should be expected ; but the British tourist's love of "tipping" is hard to restrain. Strangers are allowed to visit the principal rooms of the Castle when the family are from home, and at other times to inspect the *Chapel*, exhibiting details both of Decorated and Perpendicular, and enlivened with some modern stained glass. Beneath it is a vault or dungeon where a skeleton was discovered during alterations. Above, a stairway leads up to the tower, and the stone lantern, erroneously called *St. Michael's Chair*, which should be ascended for a noble panorama of the Cornish coast and the wide-spreading Channel. It is said by the gossips that the husband or wife who first sits in St. Michael's Chair will obtain the highly-prized privilege supposed to be conferred also by the first draught of the waters of St. Keyne's Well ; but here the feat seems a little difficult, not to say dangerous, for nervous brides. The real "St. Michael's Chair" is a rude crag on the west side of the rock.

> "Who knows not Michael's mount and chair, the pilgrim's
>   holy vaunt ;
> Both land and island twice a day, both fort and port of
>   haunt?"

There is a neat new church in the town ; and the churchyard of the old parish church of *St. Hilary* (burned and rebuilt) is, says the Rev. W. S. Lach-Szyrma, one of the most interesting in England, for "here one can see at a glance parochial remains, nearly *in situ*, within a few yards, from the age of Constantine the Great to Victoria ; *i.e.* the whole range of the history of the Christian Church in Great Britain, a period of 1570 years." The spire of this church, a mile east, is one of the few spires in Cornwall.

PENZANCE AND THE LAND'S END

To Helston by the Coast.—The country behind Marazion is somewhat uninteresting; but a fine walk or sail of some ten miles may be taken along the coast to *Porthleven* or *Looe Pool*, where we touch the limit of our exploration from the Lizard.

The village street, becoming a road, leads us out upon a prospect of broken ground and rugged cliffs, with a good back view upon the Mount. The high road soon turns inland; but one can keep on more or less near the coast. The first village is **Perranuthnoe**, from the high ground above which are more extended prospects. The church has some good features in its altar and sanctuary, its ancient font and carved figure of St. Peter. Towards the dark cliff of *Cudden Point*, stands the modern *Acton Castle*. Beyond Cudden Point the shore curves in among the rocks to form the caverned recess of **Bessie's Cove**. In the largest cavern a natural shaft, or tunnel, ascends to the surface of the cliff.

Prussia Cove is now tenanted by coastguardsmen and fishermen, in summer often visited by excursionists for its very fine fern-arched caves, and the beach studded with various kinds of sea anemones. It takes its name from a host of the former "King of Prussia" inn here, a daring smuggler who, towards the end of last century, carried his lawlessness so far as to erect a battery on the cliff, and to fire upon a man-of-war, that then made short work of the contraband stronghold.

Sidney Cove is the site of the abandoned Mount's Bay Consols Mine.

Pengersick—or *Pen-giveras-ike*, "the head fort of the Cove"—consists of two embattled towers, the remains of a castellated pile erected in the reign of Henry VIII., by one Milliton, who, in repentance of a secret murder, secluded himself here for many years. Still more romantic legends haunt these lonely walls, on which may yet be traced curious paintings, carvings, and inscriptions. Below the castle lies a wide stretch of sand; and beyond we come to *Trewavas Head*, a fine mass of granite, where are noticeable a Raised Beach and the pillar-like *Bishop's Rock*.

The next bend of the coast brings us to **Porthleven** (*Commercial Inn*), with a harbour that may claim to be the most southerly in England, but has the disadvantage of being difficult of access in stormy weather. The place seems to be a rising resort for summer visitors, but will hardly detain tourists.

Hence it is under two miles to the *Looe Pool*; but the shingly

PENZANCE

beach makes no good walking, and *Helston* can be more quickly attained by road.

The high road from Marazion to Helston, straighter and shorter, passes under *Tregoning Hill* and near the village of **Germoe**, said to have been founded about 460, by an Irish king, named Germochas; where are to be seen a very old Font, and among other uncommon features of the church a puzzling structure outside known as *St. Germoe's Chair*; then by **Breage** (pronounced *Bregue*) also ascribed to Irish enterprise, its founder having been St. Breaca, whose church has a fine tower, besides ancient frescoes of the 15th century — of our Lord and St. Christopher (gigantic), St. Michael, St. Corentin, etc.

The road, in the other direction, from Marazion to Penzance (3 m.) is flat and not very interesting. After the first mile the railway cuts it off from the sea, though on the other side of the line there is a shore walk between two crossings that may be taken when a red flag does not proclaim it occupied as a rifle range. To the right are seen the villages of *Ludgvan* and *Gulval*. We enter Penzance by the docks and the railway station.

PENZANCE.

HOTELS.—*Queen's, Mount's Bay*, on the Esplanade; *Western, Union*, in the town; *Star* and *Railway* Inns; *Perrow's, Paul's* Temperance Hotels, etc.
BOARDING-HOUSES.—*Beachfield, Dingley's*, on the Esplanade; *Melbourne House*, Alexandra Road; *Marine Mansion*, Morrab Road.

This is one of the several places which, from a certain point of view, might claim to be the most important in Cornwall. It is clearly that best known to strangers. Its own population makes over 12,000, considerably increased by the adjacent fishing villages of Newlyn and Mousehole; and we are not sure but that, excluding in each case doubtful suburbs, it is, or will soon be, the largest town of the county, if Camborne starve on the mining depression. Yet Penzance has no claim to antiquity, principally dating from the reign of Charles II., when it was made a coinage town. In 1595, it was sacked by the Spaniards, who landed at Mousehole, destroyed that village and Newlyn, and set Penzance on fire. Having thus accomplished an old Cornish prophecy, which is said to have predicted that strangers would here bring about this very

PENZANCE AND THE LAND'S END

calamity, they were fiercely attacked by the townsmen, and compelled to retire. In 1646 the town was ravaged by the Roundheads under Fairfax. Ever since the railway was made, it has been coming into repute as a winter station for invalids.

Having thus briefly disposed of its history, we proceed to outline the geography of Penzance. Lying on a declivity at the north-west edge of Mount's Bay, encircled by low hills on the north and east, it has four chief streets meeting crosswise at the *Market-Place*, blocked up by a *Market House*, at one end of which will be found an ancient cross built into the wall, and at the other a marble statue of *Sir Humphry Davy*, who now stands as the centre of his native place, looking down upon a scene that, on market days, is a very lively one in its motley concourse of farmers, fisher-folk, and miners. Here, on the left of *Market Jew Street*, by which we have mounted from the station, is the *Post Office*. To the left we turn down *Chapel Street* for the harbour, and for the oldest church, *St. Mary's*, erected in 1835 on the site of the chapel of Our Lady, relics of which, the alms-box and a small font, are preserved. The top of the tower affords an extensive view of the surrounding country. Daily service is held in this church, which has a good organ and peal of bells.

St. Paul's, Clarence Street, erected 1843, of cut and rubble granite, in the style of the 13th century, and *St. John's*, 1881, in the Early English style, near the station, are to the right of Market Jew Street, from which, at the *Market House*, we can take *Causewayhead* to gain the upper quarter, where the most prominent building is that of the West Cornwall Infirmary in *St. Clare Street* leading to the cricket ground.

If *Market Jew Street* be the Cheapside of Penzance, its prolongation, *Alverton Street*, soon brings us into what may be considered the Pall Mall or Piccadilly quarter. *Clarence Street* goes off to the right, and to the left *Morrab Road*, in and about which lodgings of the best kind may be looked for. Just beyond Clarence Street, appears on the right the fine granite block of the *Public Buildings*, opened a generation ago. The right wing contains the *Guild Hall* and other offices of the Corporation. *St. John's Hall*, in the centre, with a good organ, is used for lectures, concerts, and meetings. Here also are the Penzance *News Rooms* and *Institute, Chess Room*, etc. The left wing is appropriated to the *Royal Geological Society of Cornwall*, which gives free admission to its museum and library. In a different

PENZANCE

part of the edifice, the *Natural History and Antiquarian Society* has its collections, including a fine one of aquatic birds and rare birds of passage shot in the neighbourhood ; also models of the many interesting antiquities to be sought out around Penzance.

Near the head of *Morrab Road* will be found another group of educational institutions in the *Free Library*, the *School of Art*, and *Art Museum* (open daily : small charge on Mondays, Thursdays, and Fridays) ; then, next door, the *Mining and Science Schools*. Near the bottom of this road, to the left, bloom the *Morrab Gardens*, acquired a few years ago for public use, where *Morrab House* now contains the *Public Library*, an unusually valuable one for such a town, since besides a large selection of general literature, it includes many rare volumes, in the late Mr. Halliwell-Phillips' legacy of antiquarian, dramatic, and Shakespearian works ; Mr. Pedler's important collection of philological volumes ; and another bequeathed by the Rev. John Orme, rich in patristic, theological, and general ecclesiastic lore. It will be seen that visitors of scholarly and scientific tastes are not likely to find time hang heavy on their hands at Penzance. To the library they are admitted on a monthly subscription.

The vegetation of the gardens shows us how well qualified this place is to be a winter haven. Below the Morrab quarter, we come down upon the *Esplanade*, where Penzance, looking out across the narrow head of the bay in an unfinished but not inelegant sea front, with *Newlyn* and *Mousehole* facing it from the opposite shore, makes a somewhat feebler attempt to be a summer resort also. The bathing on the shingly beach is not very good, especially at low water ; but at the head of the Esplanade will be found excellent *Public Baths*, with sea-water swimming basin and other accommodations. Near this, *Alexandra Road*, another new thoroughfare where strangers might look for quarters, leads up to the line of *Alverton Street*, all about which we are now in genteel suburbs. Returning along the Esplanade, a very pleasant stroll or lounge on a sunny day, we reach the *Battery*, where at the end of the rock is the *Swimming Place*. Beyond, we come into the stir of the Docks. In this neighbourhood, if anywhere in the town, as in the surrounding villages, will still be kept up the curious customs of St. John's Eve, which once made much copy for guide-books, when there was a general blaze of torches, tar barrels, and bonfires, and people ran about celebrating mysteries, the origin of which they

PENZANCE AND THE LAND'S END

no longer understood ; but, whether sun-worship or Druidism, or what not, be at the bottom of it, young Christians gladly take any excuse for noise and excitement.

We do not mean to insinuate that Penzance is not a good place for summer quarters. On the contrary, its own attractions and those of the neighbourhood are such, that it will never want for visitors ; and if it be less bracing than Margate or Matlock, it is often cooler in the hot weather. But its strong point is as a winter refuge for weak chests and throats, when, in spite of the frequent rain, we have it on the authority of Sir James Clark, that there is no other place in England where invalids can spend so much time out of doors. It may be there are other Cornish nooks with just as mild and relaxing a climate ; but no other has laid itself out for winter patients so well as Penzance. For some, the Lelant *Golf-Links* are not one of its least attractions ; for others, the surrounding scenery will be enough. But among available pastimes, skating is not to be looked for unless once in a way every ten years or so.

The immediate neighbourhood of the town is what the French would call a well *accidented* oasis, the outline varied and wooded, the soil of extraordinary fertility, which, with the help of the mild winters, produces a crop of early vegetables, potatoes and broccoli in particular, that make no small part of its dealings with London and less favoured regions. Grapes, tomatoes, and asparagus are largely grown under glass. On a March Good Friday, we have seen the station almost blocked up with boxes of flowers going to London for Easter, most of which, however, probably came from the Scilly Isles. There are many seats and villas in the vicinity, whose gardens would be a pleasant sight for those fortunate enough to gain admittance, several of them belonging to members of the Bolitho family, a name figuring here as that of Fox at Falmouth.

Beyond the limits of this sheltered strip, Nature shows a more hard and wrinkled face, which yet often breaks into a smile, even among impressively frowning features. Though there are richly-wooded spots in the hollows, the general character of this country is such, that winter makes not so much difference to its rugged charms. Dull weather seems in harmony with its dark open moorlands, broken here and there by stone walls and fields of black earth, or by the lonely group of farm buildings on some ridge, or by the far-seen square church tower standing out pro-

ENVIRONS OF PENZANCE

minently as landmark of a treeless coast. Never are the Atlantic's broken battlements seen to such advantage as when a winter storm rages against the caverned base of those piles of roughly square blocks, which seem to have been heaped up by giants, poised upon each other as if a touch could send them crashing in ruin. On a fine calm autumn afternoon, when the sun shines over the sea upon the gray cliffs adorned with bright patches of lichen, and the turfy paths winding among brown bracken and brambles, and the clumps of gorse still gay with their hardy bloom, one might almost forget the flight of the seasons, as, on a genial March day when youngsters may sometimes be seen bathing in the sea, one is here easily cheated into believing that summer has really come. There are many picturesque bays and ravines, with little fishing villages hidden away in them, haunted by artists. The "Newlyn school" of painters is well known as having exploited the beauties of this neighbourhood, and made them familiar in London exhibitions. The sterner charms of the Land's End, described by so many pens, have been often pictured in our imagination, and, once seen, will not easily be forgotten.

As our rule is, we will first indicate the shorter outings to be made round the town, for which Mr. Cornish's local Guide would be found useful.

1. Madron, $2\frac{1}{2}$ miles north-west, is the mother-church of St. Penzance. The road goes out by the cemetery, then crosses meadowy uplands. To the right lies *Ilea* (pronounced *Hay*) *Moor*, where the *Wesley Rock Chapel* enshrines the granite rock from which John Wesley proclaimed the gospel to the wondering Cornishmen. Madron *Church*, 350 feet above the sea, is Early English in character, and contains some old memorials. A tombstone commemorates *George Daniell*, the founder of the schools—

> " Belgia me birth, Britaine me breeding gave,
> Cornwall a wife, ten children, and a grave."

Remark the wayside cross in the neighbouring hedge, and look for its pedestal in the village street.

Madron Well, 1 mile north, is a chalybeate well, once highly esteemed for its curative property in cases of lameness and scrofula, and its prophetical powers in respect to love and marriage, tested by young men and maidens, who on the first Sunday of May still drop rush stalks pinned cross-wise into its waters, and read

PENZANCE AND THE LAND'S END

in the bubbles their future fates. But another well, now dry, seems to be the one whose sacred character is shown by the mouldering walls of the ancient Baptistery close by, veiled in trailing ivy, mosses, lichens, and parasitical climbers. From Madron to *Lanyon Cromlech*, or the *Giant's Quoit*, is some twenty minutes' walk, from which we may turn aside, a little to the left, for the fine pile of rocks called *Trengwainton Carn*. The upper slab of the cromlech is 18 feet long, its breadth 8 feet, and three rude masses of stone about 5½ feet high support it. A similar cromlech may be seen in a field adjacent to Lanyon Farm. Farther on, some way up the road from Madron, to the right, are the *Men-an-Tol*, or Holed Stone, and the remarkable *Men Scryffa*, or Written Stone, 8 feet long, bearing the inscription—*Rialobran Cunova Fil*. Standing here, and looking towards the east, the tourist will just be able to discern the *Bosednan Ring*, or sacred Druidical arch, 68 feet in diameter, composed of eleven stones, three of which now lie upon the sward. The Men-an-Tol has been supposed to have been used for initiation, though some regard it as a rude sun-dial for calculating the solstice. Who the Rialobran, or the Cunoval or Cymbeline of the Men Scryffa was none can tell. An interesting inquiry has been made into these subjects in the *Revue Celtique* of Paris. The stone circle of the "Nine Maidens," and the picturesque abandonment of the old *Ding-Dong* Mine, should also be sought out in the same vicinity.

By this time we are well on across the promontory, where the road through Madron would bring us to *Morvah* on the "North Sea," as it is called here. Returning from Madron, one might take a pretty path by *Rose Hill* and the grounds of *Castle Horneck*, which leads into the *Alverton* quarter of Penzance. Or by the beautiful scenes of *Trereife* (pronounced *Treeve*) and *Tolcarne*, we might pass round to *Newlyn*, which would be a divagation of only a couple of miles or so.

2. To **Trevaylor**, etc. Behind the station is the pleasant suburb of *Chyandour*, and the circular camp of *Lescudjack*, which gives a good view over the town. Here also are some of the fine villas and gardens which ornament Penzance. From *Chyandour*, or up *Causewayhead* and by *Trannack Lane*, we could reach the mansion of *Trevaylor*, about as far out as Madron. Opposite the gate, a path runs down to the wooded *Trevaylor Bottoms*, where a very pretty walk may be taken up the stream to rejoin the road at *New Mill* (Inn), a mile or two beyond which the Crom-

lech called *Mulfra Quoit*, and some ancient hut circles are to be found on the left. If, having been tempted so far, one cared to push on, one could thus cross to *Zennor*, or to *Gurnard's Head*.

3. Through Chyandour, also, to the right, we may come to **Gulval**, or reach it by a path turning off through the fields soon after we get clear of houses on the *Marazion Road*. Here we pass over one of the garden lands of Cornwall. There need be no fear of missing the way, for on the hill rises the tower of *Gulval Church*, distinguished by some Early English details, and a curious inscription on the belfry wall, not to speak of an ancient cross in the churchyard, which in Cornwall, indeed, is hardly a distinction. The churchyard and the vicarage garden, with their show of exotics, testify to the mildness of the climate.

We may climb to the mossy rocks of *Gulval Carn* for the sake of the sea-view which their elevated position commands, and turning off to the north-east make across the fields to **Ludgvan**, where the erudite and amiable *Borlase* (1696-1772), historian of Cornwall, was rector for fifty-two years. There are memorials in the interior of the old Norman Church to members of the Davy family. The well of St. Ludgvan has this charm, that no one baptized in it comes to be hanged, a privilege belonging to several sacred springs of Cornwall, where it would have been more to the purpose to insure against drowning. Facing now to the north-west, we catch sight of the rugged outline of *Castle-an-Dinas*, a tower and an ancient camp on its summit, under which, either by Ludgvan or from Gulval, we might hold on to St. Ives (see p. 148). The road between *Gulval* and *Ludgvan* is about 2 miles.

4. To *Newlyn* and *Mousehole*, is *the* walk of Penzance, by a beautiful terraced road along the coast, which might be called a continuation of the Esplanade. At low tide one can cross the beach at the head of the bay, else pass through the village of *Street-an-Nowan*. Opposite a clump of cottages called *Wherry Town*, a Cornish miner, one Thomas Curtis, sank a mine 720 feet from the shore, forcing his iron shafts into the porphyritic rock 100 feet beneath the waves. Considerable quantities of ore had been raised, when the machinery was accidentally destroyed by a ship which had drifted from her moorings (1798). An unsuccessful attempt was made to re-open the mine in 1836.

Newlyn (*Red Lion Inn*) is a large fishing village, almost a suburb of Penzance, best known to the outer world by the works of the so-called "Newlyn School" of artists, who here form a

PENZANCE AND THE LAND'S END

sociable colony, and keep up a dramatic club, sometimes giving public performances for charitable purposes. The main feature of this school is a Belgian or Parisian treatment. Among its best-known members are Mr. and Mrs. Stanhope Forbes, Messrs. Bramley, Craft, Langley, Garstin, and Gotch. Thanks to Mr. Passmore Edwards, whose name turns up in Cornwall as often as Tregeagle's, an Exhibition Gallery has been built at the Penzance end of Newlyn.

St. Peter's Church, Newlyn, is a handsome granite edifice in the valley under Tolcarne, with a terra-cotta reredos and a good deal of stained glass. There are two piers at Newlyn, and the harbour when completed will be one of the best for small craft in the West of England. The fish cellars of Newlyn deserve a visit. Much of the older part of the town is built in courts—some very quaint and picturesque. The smelting works, close at hand, make a striking contrast to the ice-making, which is another industry, as is also the artistic brass and copper beating started by Mr. Bolitho. A beautiful diversion may be made up the Newlyn Valley, or up the steep hill to Paul. Let us hold by *Penlee Point* 2 miles along the coast to the next fishing village.

Mousehole nestles in a shady hollow, opening out upon two small piers of granite, some fantastic groupings of rocks, and the glorious Bay. The Spaniards made a descent on it in 1595, and the cannon ball which killed one of its worthies, Jenkin Keigwin, is treasured as an interesting relic in a cottage opposite the *Keigwin Arms*, the only old house then spared. Off the harbour lies *St. Clement's Isle*, a mass of felspar once crowned by an oratory, which formerly gave the name of *Port Enys* to Mousehole (Enys, an island). Here died, in 1788, aged 102 years, *Dolly Pentreath*, famed as the last person known to have spoken Cornish. The *Mousehole Cavern* is not far from the village.

From Mousehole, we may take a path up to Paul above; or striking inland a little, and then turning back to the coast, the pedestrian will reach *Lamorna Cove*, a lovely nook. There, following inland the course of a small stream that ripples into the sea, we reach the high road, and gain **St. Paul**, commonly called *Paul*, a large village with an ancient church tower prominent on the heights, which command a grand view of Mount Bay to the Lizard. The remainder of the church was rebuilt after the descent of the Spanish in 1595. In the south aisle (dedicated to S. Pol de Leon, the Breton bishop who founded the parish) is

THE LAND'S END

the only extant epitaph in Cornish—to Captain Hichens. Dolly Pentreath lies buried in the churchyard, where a tomb to her memory has been erected by the philological piety of Prince Louis Lucien Bonaparte, as a monument to the old Cornish language.

From Paul back to Penzance is half an hour's walk, mostly down hill. But strangers should be aware of the charms they would find by following up the course of the stream from *Newlyn*, leading to *Trembath* Valley, and by *Buryas Bridge*, through scenery picturesque in a style less common hereabouts.

The reader may now be impatient to get on to the Land's End, for which, indeed, our last excursion has brought him well on the way; so we will only wait to say that in summer many pleasant excursions may be taken by cars running to *Helston*, *Gurnard's Head*, the *Lizard*, and various points sought by strangers, not to speak of the omnibuses and vans that ply here regularly, even to places served by the railway. There are frequent steamer trips also to *St. Ives*, the *Lizard*, *Falmouth*, etc.; and here start the mail boats for the Scilly Islands. The favourite excursion is of course to the *Land's End*, for which more than one crew of excursionists start daily, in the season, at a return fare of 3s. 6d. In winter, the tourist must arrange for himself.

Before starting on the usual trip, however, let us mention that there are sixpenny omnibuses several times a day (7 m.) between Penzance and *St. Just in Penwith*, as it is formally called in distinction from its neighbour in *Roseland*, which might be taken as a centre for exploring the north coast, being 7 miles distant from the Land's End, but close to Cape Cornwall, and not far from the Botallack Mine. **St. Just** (*Commercial Inn*) is a town of miners, who call it *St. 'Oost*, and has several objects of interest of its own in the *Plan-an-Guare*, a British amphitheatre, 126 feet in diameter, once used for the miracle plays so admired by Cornishmen; in a remarkable 15th-century Church, with Tomb of Silus 1400 years old; in *St. Helen's Oratory* on Cape Cornwall; and in several ancient burrows and sacred circles of the neighbourhood.

THE LAND'S END.

The shortest road, by *Sennen* (10 m.), is not the favourite one. On the right, about 4 miles from Penzance, is **Sancreed**, whose church has recently been well restored, and the churchyard contains one of the best Cornish crosses. On the left we pass the

PENZANCE AND THE LAND'S END

Boscawen stone circle; then on the right *Chapel Carn Brea* (800 feet), and *Bartiney* rather higher, which stand up proudly as the most western hills in England. **Sennen** Church town has an inn which boasts itself on one side, "The First," and on the other "The Last Inn in England." But the modern "Land's End Hotel" may now lay claim to this distinction. The westernmost church of England, restored and well cared for, contains an ancient dated font, a mediæval statue, and a fresco of a city (probably intended for the New Jerusalem).

The most striking approach to the Land's End is from *Sennen Cove*, picturesque in itself, and a very convenient centre for tourists who wish to do the region thoroughly. There is good sea-fishing near here, and lodgings can be had.

That we may not have to return, we will briefly indicate the points of the coast between the *Land's End* and *Cape Cornwall*, along the shore of *Whitesand Bay*.

Pedn Men Dhu—i.e. "the black-rock headland." The rock at its base is named the *Irish Lady*. *Sennen Cove*—"above is the village of Sennen." *Vell an Dreath*—"the mill in the sand." *Carn Towan*—"the sandy carn." *Carn Barges*—"the kite's carn." *Carn Mellyn*—"the yellow carn." *Polpry Cove*—"the clay pit." *Carn Leskez*—"the carn of light," where the Druids, it is said, were wont to kindle their sacred fires. *Carn Glos*—"the gray rock," opposite which lie the *Brisons* or Sisters, two rocky islands off the south side of Cape Cornwall. *Priest's Cove* is close under the headland.

The more interesting road, taken by the cars one way, so as to let their passengers visit the *Logan Rock*, turns off to the left from the former for **St. Buryan** (Inn: *Ship*), whose lofty tower makes a landmark in a rather monotonous prospect. Here Athelstan, after he had subjugated the Scilly Islands, founded a college of Augustinian canons. Its fine Church, now restored, contains a coffin-shaped monument to Clarice, the wife of Geoffrey de Bolleit, and an ancient Norman arch. There was in the church a very fine Flemish screen of the Renaissance style, part of which may be seen in the vestry. There is an old cross at the entrance, and another in the churchyard, which also shows a monument to the late Mr. Augustus Smith, lord-proprietor of the Scilly Isles. This church, like *Crantock*, had at one time the rank of a collegiate one with a dean and canons.

THE LOGAN ROCK

On the left, as we continue our route, there will be observed *Boskenna*, a picturesque mansion approached by a noble arcade of beech and sycamores. Descending into the deep hollow which opens upon the sea at *Penberth Cove*, we next climb the hill to the rude little weather-beaten hamlet of *Treryn* (pronounced *Treen*), where refreshment, and, if needed, a guide may be procured. From this to the grand promontory of *Treryn Castle*, or *Treryn Dinas*, is an easy walk. Here we may observe the remains of a triple vallum and fosse, and entering within the enclosure, ascend to the celebrated **Logan Rock**, a mass of granite weighing $65\frac{1}{2}$ tons, nearly 17 feet long and 30 feet in circumference, which was formerly so poised upon its axis that it could be easily shaken, and yet soon regained its equilibrium. In 1824 it was overthrown by Lieutenant Goldsmith, a nephew of the poet, and some sailors under his command, by way of disproving the assertion of the antiquarian Borlase that no mechanical force could remove it. The Admiralty ordered Goldsmith to replace the Logan in its position, a task which he accomplished at very great cost. The stone can be rocked, but there is a way of doing it. Those who are not sure of foot and eye would do well to wonder from below.

The road we have come is about 9 miles. The pedestrian might have reached the same point more deviously, yet agreeably, leaving Penzance by way of *Paul Hill* and the *Lamorna Valley*, near the head of which is a curious artificial cave known as the *Fogou* or *Fog-hole*, where some Cavaliers were hidden in 1646. Having climbed the ascent to *Bolleit*, or *Boleigh* (a farmstead)—the "place of blood"—scene of Athelstan's defeat of the Britons in 936, on the right of the road, you now pass two upright stones, 12 and 16 feet high, one in each field, called "the Pipers"; and farther on, after passing a blacksmith's shop, come on an ancient cross and the *Holed* stone (both on the road). The latter is said to have been used by the Druids for tying down their human sacrifices. In a field to the left of this is the circle called the "Merry Maidens," consisting of nineteen upright stones, and measuring 30 paces in diameter. A footpath across the field, from the smithy, leads the visitor right through the circle, and joins the road just at the "holed" stone. These poor merry maidens, like other untimely revellers of old Cornwall and Devon, were turned into stone for dancing on Sunday. Near *St. Just* there is a circle with the same name and legend.

PENZANCE AND THE LAND'S END

Hence one can strike to the right, and follow a tolerable road into the church-town of *St. Buryan*, from which the carriage route may be followed. But some might prefer to hold on by the shorter road to *Penberth*, even if they did not care to follow the coast all the way from Lamorna, by *Boscawen Point, St. Loy's Cove*, the Mermaid's Cave of *Porthguarnon, Merthen Point, Penberth Cove*, and *Cribba Head*, beyond which we come to the Logan Rock. For driving to the Land's End, the road now cuts across inland, 3 or 4 miles, by barren moors and scattered hamlets. But though the distance is twice as far, it would be a pity to lose the chance of walking round this corner, which many judge the finest cliff scenery in Cornwall.

The first point is the pretty little cove of **Porthcurnow**, whose sand, formed of comminuted shells, and often dotted with fine unbroken specimens, invites one to a bathe that may be had in retired nooks, where the modest swimmer is little likely to be surprised unless by sympathising youths. For here is the landing-place of more than one Telegraph Cable ; and in the ravine behind are the buildings of the *Eastern Telegraph Company's Station*, a school where cadets are trained to use the delicate instruments required to deal with feeble electric currents passing hundreds of miles under the ocean. The station with its dependencies is perhaps the largest, certainly the most imposing, place in the parish, as its young garrison form the most lively part of the population. They call themselves the "Exiles," and profess to bemoan their lonely lot ; but what with football, cricket, billiards, even a theatre and occasional balls, seem to have not a bad time of it by help of hearty British pastimes such as they may miss in the distant foreign posts for which their duty destines them. In their off-hours the free and easy flannels and blazers of these castaways are much in evidence about the country, strewn with shreds of the cabalistically marked tape which make the main object of their study.

The signalling instrument used here is the *Siphon Recorder*, which, like a stylograph pen, traces a thin line of ink upon an endless type ; then this line, deflected to right or left, takes a wavy form, like the outline of a mountain chain on a rude map, which deflections answer to the dots and dashes that are the commoner signs of the Morse alphabet. It takes some learning to spell out these silent signals ; and

ST. LEVAN

visitors, courteously admitted to inspection, will be impressed, if not instructed, by the wonderful devices of science which to the uninitiated seem nothing short of mysterious. It is told how an old farmer and his wife could not restrain their amazement when the working of the Siphon Recorder had been duly explained. "Dear me!" said the good woman, "and does that tape come all the way from Spain?" "No, you fool," the husband rebuked her, in the pride of masculine intelligence. "Of course it is only the ink that comes from Spain."

The Atlantic cable that takes the water at Sennen is worked by the *Mirror Galvanometer*, in which a small mirror fitted with light magnets and suspended by a silk thread, is made to reflect a ray of light to right or left with every motion caused by the currents.

Above *Porthcurnow*, inland to the west, stands retiringly in a hollow the Church of St. Levan, small and solitary godfather of several surrounding hamlets. There is some very remarkable carving inside, and a fine old cross in the churchyard, which has also a *lych stone* for resting coffins on. Nearer the sea will be found traces of the *Baptistery* of St. Levan, who, like other Cornish saints, had a holy well of his own.

Lodgings can be had, but not many of them, at farms in this neighbourhood, which would be a most enjoyable sojourn for a week or two if one did not mind post and papers being rather late in arrival.

We regain the cliffs to follow them steadily henceforth to the Land's End, noting the main features, but begging the tourist to remember that we do not attempt even to name all the points, caverns, gullies, fissures, and lichen-stained rock masses in which this corner is so rich. By *Manack Point—i.e.* "the Monk's Point," *Pedn Mean an Mor*—"the headland of stone in the sea," *Carn Vesacks*—"the rock outside," and *Pol Ledan*—"the broad pool," we come to **Porthgwarra**—the "higher port," a fishing village at the entrance of a deep ravine that sometimes gives harbour to artists. There is a curious tunnel here through which boats are launched into the sea. Beyond, are *Polostoc*—"the cap headland," as resembling a fisherman's cap ; the *Ella Rock* island ; then comes the point which some call the finest in Cornwall.

Tol Pedn Penwith—that is, the "Holed Headland" in Penwith, is named from its *Funnel Rock*, a pit or chasm, about 100 feet in depth and 8 feet in diameter, cut apparently as smooth as a wall might be, from the slope of the cliff to the sea roaring below. The bottom of the funnel can be visited at

PENZANCE AND THE LAND'S END

low water. The *Chair Ladder* is another remarkable feature of the cliff. The *Rundlestone* lies off this point about 1 mile, its position indicated to mariners by the two conical beacons placed on the headland. Numerous disastrous wrecks have nevertheless occurred in this vicinity.

From *Tol Pedn Penwith* we go on towards *Pardenick Point*, its rival in grandeur, passing successively *Porth Looe*, a rocky cove, which, quiet as it looks, has also been the scene of shipwrecks; *Carn Barra*, the "loaf-carn," a fantastic mass of rock; *Zawn Kellys*, the "Fallen Cave"; *Mill Bay* or *Nanjissel Cove*, "the Cove under the Vale," one of the most romantic points on this romantic coast; the chasm called "The Song of the Sea"; *Carn Voel*, the "Chilly Carn"; *Zawn Ruth*, the "Red Cave"; *Mozrang Pool*, the "Maid's Pool," a sheltered recess in the shadow of **Pardenick**, "the hill upon hill," that striking promontory where the Titans would seem to have been surprised by the Gods while erecting a huge palace for their king.

Beyond this comes the island of *Enys Dodman*, sometimes visited by boat for the sake of its rock archway. Off *Carn Greab*, the "Cock's Comb Rock," lies a group of rocks, the *Guelaz*, some of which bear fantastic resemblances to natural objects. One of the most conspicuous is known as the *Armed Knight*. A mass of granite on the side of another carn here is called *Dr. Johnson's Head*. Again and again we have been deceived by the resemblance of the rocks to hewn shapes, while we are often astonished how such nicely poised masses could have taken their place without human handiwork.

And now we reach our goal, marked by a little group of buildings, over which predominates the *Land's End Hotel*, recently enlarged in sign of a thriving business. Our experience has been to find it inhospitably closed in winter. A humbler place of refreshment also does a good trade in the excursion season, when the sentimental visitor is little like to enjoy the scene in congenial solitude.

The **Land's End**, 293 miles from London, the *Bolerium* of the ancient geographers, and the western extremity of England, is a point of horridly broken granite, roofed by turf and pierced by a cavern, its extremity crumbled into huge boulders and foaming reefs. From the cliffs above its height may seem insignificant, but it commands a grand prospect. Over a mile from the shore rises the tall shaft of the *Longships Lighthouse*. The

THE LAND'S END

insulated rock on which it stands is 60 feet high, and the granite building itself 52 feet. Some miles to the south another dangerous point is marked by the *Wolf Lighthouse*. To the north extends the curve of *Whitesand Bay*, bounded by *Cape Cornwall*.

Though a sufficiently striking point, the interest of this famous spot is rather sentimental than picturesquely magnificent, and some may complain that Old England does not end off in a more bold and imposing manner. "Those who expect," says the author of *A Londoner's Walk to the Land's End*, "to see a towering or far-stretching promontory will be disappointed. We form our ideas from ordinary maps, and imagine England's utmost cape to be a narrow tongue thrust out from the firm shore, along which we may walk to meet the advancing waves. But we find the reality to be merely a protruding shoulder or buttress of the vast irregular bluff that terminates the county. Cape Cornwall, which looks so grand about 2 miles distant, appears to extend farther to the west than the Land's End."

But here is the end of Cornwall, of which we now take leave, unless for a visit to the scattered Scilly Isles, that from this nearest point, some 25 miles away, may or may not be seen reposing like light clouds against the western sky.

Pilchard Fishery.—The pilchard, though not very different in size and other respects from a herring or from a large sardine, is almost peculiar to the Cornwall coast, living habitually in deep water not far west of the Scilly Isles, and visiting the coast in great shoals. Twelve millions of pilchards are said to have been taken in a single day; and the indications of such a great army of fish passing the Land's End, pursued by hordes of dog-fish, hake, and cod, besides vast flocks of sea-birds, is the buried treasure of a St. Ives boy's dream. When brought to shore the pilchards are carried to the cellars to be cured. They are then packed in hogsheads, each containing about 2400 fish. These casks are largely exported to Naples and other Italian ports—whence the fishermen's toast, "Long life to the Pope, and death to thousands!" Spanish customers, from a mistaken idea of their being smoked, called them *fumados*, hence the Cornish name "fair maids."

The pilchards are expected off the coast in October, when their appearance gives rise to general excitement at a place like St. Ives. Often have been described the patient watching of the *huers* on the cliffs, who with a huge trumpet at length announce their joyful discovery, and by the waving of bushes telegraph the movements of the shoal marked by the colour of the sea and its hovering escort of gulls; the rush of men, women, and children to the shore with shouts of *heva! heva!* which is Cornish for the classic *Eureka;* the marshalling of the seine boats; the shooting of the huge nets; the enclosure of the luckless victims by myriads; then the hurried orgy of capturing, pickling and storing, stimulated by its promise of prosperity to the whole place.

These exciting scenes have been to some extent superseded by what is really the old method of drift-net fishing, where the boats, by night, go out farther to sea to meet their prey, and the incidents are not so dramatic if the results prove more satisfactory. The drift fishing is accused by some old people of frightening away the pilchards from less fortunately placed stations, perhaps on the same principle as Tenterden Steeple was the cause of Goodwin Sands. It is certain that they no longer favour parts of the coast where once their yearly coming brought no small gain. The manner of curing also has changed, the old way of drysalting having given place to pickling in tanks of brine, which, it appears, cannot be profitably done except on a large scale; then often an enormous catch goes to waste for want of proper means to deal with it, and the windfall of the sea is turned into manure for the land. The new way of pickling does not seem to recommend itself to Italian tastes, for the Cornishmen are losing hold on their best market. Perhaps they have their own fault to blame: we have heard of a case where a cellarful of bad fish, condemned by the officer of health as a nuisance, was shipped off as fit food for the benighted foreigners, who keep their Popish fasts to fill British stomachs. At all events, from one cause or another, the pilchard fishery, like the Cornish mines, is not what it once was. The gigantic haul of 1833, if we are not mistaken, turned people's heads, so that all along the coast they went in for this adventure with much the same speculative spirit shown in mining; now, too many rotting boats and nets tell a tale of disappointment. But if pilchard fishery continues profitable anywhere, it is at St. Ives. Mevagissey, as we already mentioned, deals largely in that small variety known as the Cornish sardine. The real sardine, it appears, shows a disposition to fight shy of the French and Portuguese coasts; and any ill wind that kept him permanently absent there, would blow nothing but good to Cornwall, whose old toast of the three F's—" fish, tin, and copper!"—is not at present a very rousing one.

Besides pilchards, mackerel are taken in large numbers on the southern coast. Conger eels of great size, weighing from 60 to 120 lbs., are found near the shores, and among other fish should be mentioned mullet, hake, and John Dory. Readers desiring full information as to deep-sea fishing at the various points round Cornwall, may be referred to Mr. E. W. Rashleigh's *Brief Guide to Edible Cornish Fishes*, published by Mr. Wellington, Fowey.

Andrew Gill: I have collected historical photographs and optical antiques for over forty years. I am a professional 'magic lantern' showman presenting Victorian slide shows and giving talks on early optical entertainments for museums, festivals, special interest groups and universities. Please visit my website '**Magic Lantern World**' at www.magiclanternist.com

My booklets and photo albums are available from Amazon, simply search for the titles below. If you've enjoyed this book, please leave a review on Amazon, as good ratings are very important to independent authors. If you're disappointed, please let me know the reason, so that I can address the issue in future editions.

Historical travel guides
New York
Jersey in 1921
Norwich in 1880
Doon the Watter
Liverpool in 1886
Nottingham in 1899
Bournemouth in 1914
Great Yarmouth in 1880
Victorian Walks in Surrey
The Way We Were: Bath
A Victorian Visit to Brighton
The Way We Were: Lincoln
A Victorian Visit to Hastings
A Victorian Visit to Falmouth
Newcastle upon Tyne in 1903
Victorian and Edwardian York
The Way We Were: Llandudno
A Victorian Visit to North Devon
The Way We Were: Manchester
A Victorian Guide to Birmingham
Leeds through the Magic Lantern
An Edwardian Guide to Leicester
Victorian and Edwardian Bradford
Victorian and Edwardian Sheffield

The Way We Were: North Cornwall
A Victorian Visit to Fowey and Looe
A Victorian Visit to Peel, Isle of Man
Doncaster through the Magic Lantern
The Way We Were: The Lake District
Lechlade to Oxford by Canoe in 1875
Guernsey, Sark and Alderney in 1921
East Devon through the Magic Lantern
The River Thames from Source to Sea
A Victorian Visit to Ramsey, Isle of Man
A Victorian Visit to Douglas, Isle of Man
Victorian Totnes through the Magic Lantern
Victorian Whitby through the Magic Lantern
Victorian London through the Magic Lantern
St. Ives through the Victorian Magic Lantern
Victorian Torquay through the Magic Lantern
Victorian Glasgow through the Magic Lantern
The Way We Were: Wakefield and Dewsbury
The Way We Were: Hebden Bridge to Halifax
Victorian Blackpool through the Magic Lantern
Victorian Scarborough through the Magic Lantern
The Way We Were: Hull and the Surrounding Area
The Way We Were: Harrogate and Knaresborough
A Victorian Tour of North Wales: Rhyl to Llandudno
A Victorian Visit to Lewes and the surrounding area
The Isle of Man through the Victorian Magic Lantern
A Victorian Visit to Helston and the Lizard Peninsula
A Victorian Railway Journey from Plymouth to Padstow
A Victorian Visit to Barmouth and the Surrounding Area
The Way We Were: Holmfirth, Honley and Huddersfield
A Victorian Visit to Malton, Pickering and Castle Howard
A Victorian Visit to Eastbourne and the surrounding area
A Victorian Visit to Aberystwyth and the Surrounding Area
The Way We Were: Rotherham and the Surrounding Area
A Victorian Visit to Castletown, Port St. Mary and Port Erin
Penzance and Newlyn through the Victorian Magic Lantern
A Victorian Journey to Snowdonia, Caernarfon and Pwllheli
Victorian Brixham and Dartmouth through the Magic Lantern
Victorian Plymouth and Devonport through the Magic Lantern
A Victorian Tour of North Wales: Conwy to Caernarfon via Anglesey
Staithes, Runswick and Robin Hood's Bay through the Magic Lantern
Dawlish, Teignmouth and Newton Abbot through the Victorian Magic Lantern

Walking Books
Victorian Edinburgh Walks
Victorian Rossendale Walks
More Victorian Rossendale Walks

Victorian Walks on the Isle of Wight (Book 1)
Victorian Walks on the Isle of Wight (Book 2)
Victorian Rossendale Walks: The End of an Era

Other historical topics
The YMCA in the First World War
Sarah Jane's Victorian Tour of Scotland
The River Tyne through the Magic Lantern
The 1907 Wrench Cinematograph Catalogue
Victorian Street Life through the Magic Lantern
The First World War through the Magic Lantern
Ballyclare May Fair through the Victorian Magic Lantern
The Story of Burnley's Trams through the Magic Lantern
The Franco-British 'White City' London Exhibition of 1908
The 1907 Wrench 'Optical and Science Lanterns' Catalogue
The CWS Crumpsall Biscuit Factory through the Magic Lantern
How They Built the Forth Railway Bridge: A Victorian Magic Lantern Show

Historical photo albums (just photos)
The Way We Were: Suffolk
Norwich: The Way We Were
The Way We Were: Somerset
Fife through the Magic Lantern
York through the Magic Lantern
Rossendale: The Way We Were
The Way We Were: Cumberland
Burnley through the Magic Lantern
Oban to the Hebrides and St. Kilda
Tasmania through the Magic Lantern
Swaledale through the Magic Lantern
Llandudno through the Magic Lantern
Birmingham through the Magic Lantern
Penzance, Newlyn and the Isles of Scilly
Great Yarmouth through the Magic Lantern
Ancient Baalbec through the Magic Lantern
The Isle of Skye through the Magic Lantern
Ancient Palmyra through the Magic Lantern
The Kentish Coast from Whitstable to Hythe
New South Wales through the Magic Lantern
From Glasgow to Rothesay by Paddle Steamer
Victorian Childhood through the Magic Lantern
The Way We Were: Yorkshire Railway Stations
Southampton, Portsmouth and the Great Liners
Newcastle upon Tyne through the Magic Lantern
Egypt's Ancient Monuments through the Magic Lantern
The Way We Were: Birkenhead, Port Sunlight and the Wirral
Ancient Egypt, Baalbec and Palmyra through the Magic Lantern

Copyright © 2021 by Andrew Gill. All rights reserved.
No part of this book may be reproduced or used in any manner without written permission of the copyright owner.

Contact email: victorianhistory@virginmedia.com

Printed in Great Britain
by Amazon